From Rags to Riches:
The Journey to Wealth

Acknowledgments

Writing a book is not a solitary endeavor, and there are many people who have contributed to the creation of this work. I would like to express my gratitude to each of them.

Firstly, I would like to thank my family for their unwavering support and encouragement throughout this journey. Without their love and patience, this book would not have been possible.

I am also grateful to my friends and colleagues who have shared their experiences and insights with me, and who have offered valuable feedback on the early drafts of this book.

I would like to thank my editor for her guidance and expertise in helping me shape this manuscript into a cohesive and engaging book. Her attention to detail and commitment to excellence have been invaluable.

Finally, I would like to thank the readers of this book for their interest and attention. It is my hope that the stories and strategies shared in these pages will inspire and motivate you to embark on your own journey to wealth.

Thank you all.

Table of Contents

Introduction

As you read this, you may be struggling to make ends meet, living paycheck to paycheck, wondering if there is a way out of your current situation. Or perhaps you are already on a path towards financial success, but you're not quite sure how to take your wealth-building to the next level. Either way, you are not alone in your quest for financial freedom.

In this book, you will embark on a journey that will take you from the depths of poverty to the heights of prosperity. You will hear from individuals who have overcome seemingly insurmountable odds to achieve financial success, and learn from their stories of perseverance and determination. You will discover the different forms that wealth can take, and the strategies that you can use to build it, no matter where you are starting from.

But this book is not just about money. It's about the freedom that comes with financial security, the ability to pursue your passions and dreams without the constraints of financial worry. It's about creating a better future for yourself, your family, and your community.

So, if you're ready to take control of your financial destiny, to turn your rags into riches, then join us on this journey. The road may be long and challenging, but the rewards at the end will be worth it. Let's begin.

In the following chapters, we will explore the specific strategies and techniques that can help individuals build wealth, overcome financial challenges, and achieve financial freedom. Whether you're just starting out or you're looking to take your finances to the next level, the principles and strategies in this book will provide you with the tools and knowledge to achieve your financial goals and live a life of true financial freedom.

Overview of the book

"From Rags to Riches: The Journey to Wealth" is a book that explores the journey from poverty to prosperity and the importance of creating wealth. The book provides an overview of what it means to be poor and the impact poverty can have on individuals and communities. It also features personal stories of individuals who have overcome poverty and achieved financial success, as well as strategies for building wealth through entrepreneurship, investing, and saving.

The book also delves into the common challenges that individuals face on the path to wealth, such as mindset, resilience, and persistence, and provides strategies for overcoming these obstacles. It defines wealth and the different forms it can take, as well as the concept of financial freedom and what it means to different individuals.

Overall, "From Rags to Riches: The Journey to Wealth" provides a comprehensive guide for readers who are looking to create wealth and achieve financial freedom. With a combination of personal stories and practical strategies, this book serves as a source of inspiration and motivation for readers who want to transform their lives and build a better future for themselves and their families.

In addition to the above, "From Rags to Riches: The Journey to Wealth" emphasizes the importance of having a strong foundation for success. The book highlights the strategies for overcoming poverty and building a solid financial base, which is crucial in the journey to wealth creation.

The book also recognizes that building wealth is not an easy feat and involves overcoming various obstacles along the way. It provides guidance on how to overcome these challenges and encourages readers to adopt a mindset of resilience and persistence.

Furthermore, "From Rags to Riches: The Journey to Wealth" features stories of successful individuals who have achieved financial freedom through different means, such as passive income, retirement planning, and wealth management. The book provides insights into the strategies that these individuals have used to achieve financial freedom and provides inspiration for readers to follow in their footsteps.

Overall, "From Rags to Riches: The Journey to Wealth" is a practical guide that provides readers with the knowledge and tools needed to build wealth and achieve financial freedom. Through a combination of personal stories and practical strategies, readers will gain a deeper understanding of the journey to wealth creation and be empowered to take action towards building their own financial success.

Explanation of the journey from poverty to prosperity

The journey from poverty to prosperity is a challenging but rewarding process that involves overcoming various obstacles to achieve financial stability and success. Poverty can be defined as a lack of access to basic necessities such as food, shelter, and healthcare. It can also lead to social exclusion, poor education, and limited opportunities for growth and development.

To start the journey towards prosperity, individuals need to identify their strengths and develop a plan to leverage them to their advantage. This may involve acquiring new skills or education, exploring entrepreneurship, or finding ways to invest their resources wisely.

The journey to prosperity often requires significant effort and sacrifice, including taking on additional work, saving money, and making smart financial decisions. It may also involve taking risks and embracing opportunities that present themselves along the way.

As individuals work towards building wealth, they may encounter challenges and setbacks, such as economic downturns, unexpected expenses, or personal crises. However, with a mindset of resilience and perseverance, these challenges can be overcome, and individuals can continue on their path towards prosperity.

Ultimately, the journey from poverty to prosperity is a transformative process that involves not only building financial stability but also developing a sense of purpose, confidence, and empowerment. It enables individuals to create a better future for themselves and their families and contribute to the growth and development of their communities.

The journey from poverty to prosperity is not a linear path, and success may not come overnight. However, with patience, dedication, and hard work, individuals can transform their lives and achieve financial stability and success.

One important aspect of this journey is financial education. Many individuals may lack the knowledge and skills needed to manage their finances effectively and make smart financial decisions. Financial education can help individuals understand the importance of budgeting, saving, and investing, and empower them to take control of their financial future.

Another key factor in the journey from poverty to prosperity is access to resources and opportunities. This may include access to education, job training, and mentoring, as well as access to capital, credit, and financial services. Governments, non-profit organizations, and private businesses can play a critical role in providing these resources and creating an environment that supports wealth creation.

Overall, the journey from poverty to prosperity is a complex and challenging process that requires hard work, dedication, and a commitment to learning and growth. With the right mindset, tools, and resources, individuals can overcome poverty and achieve financial stability and success, transforming their lives and creating a better future for themselves and their communities.

Another important aspect of the journey from poverty to prosperity is the development of a growth mindset. A growth mindset is the belief that abilities and intelligence can be developed through hard work, dedication, and perseverance. By adopting a growth mindset, individuals can overcome limiting beliefs and self-doubt, and build the resilience needed to overcome obstacles and setbacks.

Another key factor in the journey from poverty to prosperity is building a strong support network. Support from family, friends, mentors, and community organizations can provide individuals with encouragement, advice, and guidance as they navigate the challenges of building wealth.

In addition, embracing a long-term perspective is crucial in the journey from poverty to prosperity. Wealth creation is a marathon, not a sprint, and requires individuals to think about their financial future in the long term. This means setting long-term goals, developing a plan to achieve them, and making consistent progress towards those goals over time.

Finally, the journey from poverty to prosperity is not just about building wealth for oneself, but also about contributing to the greater good. Wealth creation can have a positive impact on individuals, families, and communities, and individuals can use their resources to give back and make a difference in the world.

In summary, the journey from poverty to prosperity is a multi-faceted process that involves developing a growth mindset, accessing resources and opportunities, building a strong support network, embracing a long-term perspective, and contributing to the greater good. Through hard work, dedication, and a commitment to personal growth and development, individuals can transform their lives and achieve financial stability and success.

Importance of creating wealth

Creating wealth is an essential aspect of achieving financial stability and success. Wealth creation enables individuals to achieve their goals, provide for their families, and contribute to their communities. In this section of the book, we will discuss the importance of creating wealth and the benefits that come with it.

Firstly, creating wealth provides individuals with financial security. It allows them to have a safety net in case of unexpected expenses or emergencies. This can help to reduce stress and anxiety and provide peace of mind knowing that they have the resources to handle unexpected situations.

Secondly, creating wealth allows individuals to achieve their personal and financial goals. Whether it's buying a home, starting a business, or saving for retirement, building wealth can provide individuals with the financial resources needed to achieve their aspirations.

Thirdly, creating wealth provides individuals with the ability to support their families and loved ones. It allows them to provide for their children's education, invest in their future, and ensure that their loved ones are taken care of financially.

Fourthly, creating wealth enables individuals to give back to their communities. By supporting charitable organizations and contributing to social causes, individuals can make a positive impact on the world and help to create a better future for all.

Finally, creating wealth provides individuals with the ability to enjoy life and pursue their passions. Whether it's traveling, pursuing hobbies, or spending time with loved ones, building wealth can provide individuals with the financial freedom to enjoy life to the fullest.

In conclusion, creating wealth is an essential aspect of achieving financial stability and success. It provides individuals with financial security, the ability to achieve their personal and financial goals, the ability to support their families and loved ones, the opportunity to give back to their communities, and the freedom to enjoy life. In the following chapters of this book, we will discuss strategies and tools for building wealth and achieving financial success.

In order to create wealth, it's important to understand the fundamental principles of financial management. This includes developing a budget, managing debt, saving for emergencies, and investing for the future.

Developing a budget is the first step towards financial stability and success. A budget is a financial plan that outlines an individual's income, expenses, and savings goals. It allows individuals to track their spending, identify areas where they can cut back, and allocate their resources towards their financial goals.

Managing debt is another crucial aspect of financial management. Debt can be a useful tool for achieving certain goals, such as buying a home or starting a business. However, too much debt can be a burden and hinder wealth creation. By managing debt effectively, individuals can reduce their interestpayments, improve their credit score, and free up more resources for saving and investing.

Saving for emergencies is also important in building wealth. Unexpected expenses, such as medical bills or car repairs, can derail financial progress if individuals don't have adequate savings to cover them. By setting aside a portion of their income for emergencies, individuals can protect themselves from financial shocks and ensure that they stay on track towards their financial goals.

Finally, investing for the future is a critical aspect of wealth creation. Investing allows individuals to grow their wealth over time and take advantage of the power of compounding. By investing in stocks, bonds, real estate, or other assets, individuals can build wealth and achieve their financial goals over the long term.

In the following chapters of this book, we will delve into these topics in greater detail, providing practical advice and strategies for managing money, reducing debt, building savings, and investing for the future. With the right tools and knowledge, individuals can take control of their finances and create a brighter financial future for themselves and their families.

In addition to the fundamental principles of financial management, there are also mindset and behavior shifts that can help individuals on their journey to wealth creation.

One key mindset shift is moving from a scarcity mindset to an abundance mindset. A scarcity mindset is characterized by fear, anxiety, and a sense of lack, while an abundance mindset is characterized by positivity, gratitude, and a belief in one's own potential. By adopting an abundance mindset, individuals can approach their finances with confidence and optimism, and be more open to opportunities for growth and success.

Another behavior shift that can aid in wealth creation is focusing on value creation. Instead of solely focusing on how to make money, individuals should look for ways to create value for others. By identifying and addressing the needs and wants of others, individuals can build successful businesses, create innovative products, and provide valuable services that can lead to financial success.

It's also important to practice discipline and delayed gratification. Wealth creation is not a quick or easy process, and it requires a willingness to sacrifice short-term pleasures for long-term gain. This might mean cutting back on expenses, staying disciplined with savings and investing, and resisting the temptation to make impulsive purchases.

Finally, it's essential to surround oneself with supportive and like-minded individuals. This can include family members, friends, mentors, and professional advisors who can offer encouragement, advice, and support on the journey to wealth creation.

By adopting these mindset and behavior shifts, individuals can set themselves up for success on their journey from rags to riches. In the following chapters of this book, we will provide practical tips and strategies for implementing these shifts and building wealth over the long term.

Defining poverty and its impact on individuals and communities

Before we can fully understand the journey from poverty to prosperity, we must first define what poverty is and how it impacts individuals and communities.

Poverty is typically defined as a lack of access to basic necessities, including food, shelter, and healthcare. It is also characterized by a lack of resources and opportunities, such as education, job training, and financial services. Poverty can be both absolute and relative, meaning that it can be measured by an individual's level of income or by the level of income within a particular community or region.

Poverty can have a significant impact on individuals and communities. It can lead to poor health outcomes, limited access to education and job opportunities, and social exclusion. It can also perpetuate cycles of poverty and inequality, as individuals who grow up in poverty often struggle to escape it and pass it on to future generations.

In addition, poverty can have broader economic and social consequences. It can limit economic growth and development, reduce productivity, and increase social tensions and instability. This can lead to a range of negative outcomes, including increased crime rates, political unrest, and reduced social cohesion.

Despite the challenges associated with poverty, there are many examples of individuals and communities that have successfully overcome it and achieved prosperity. In the following chapters of this book, we will explore some of these success stories and provide practical advice and strategies for individuals who are seeking to improve their financial situations and escape the cycle of poverty.

To fully understand the impact of poverty, it's important to examine the different forms it can take. Absolute poverty refers to a lack of access to basic necessities, while relative poverty is defined as a lack of access to the same level of resources and opportunities as others in society.

In developing countries, absolute poverty is often characterized by extreme deprivation, including lack of access to clean water, adequate nutrition, and basic healthcare. In developed countries, absolute poverty may still exist, but it is typically less severe and may manifest as homelessness or a lack of access to basic healthcare.

Relative poverty, on the other hand, is characterized by a lack of access to the same resources and opportunities as others in society. This can manifest as a lack of access to education, job opportunities, or financial services. It can also be influenced by social factors, such as discrimination, social exclusion, and cultural norms.

The impact of poverty can be especially severe on children. Children who grow up in poverty are more likely to experience poor health outcomes, perform poorly in school, and face limited job opportunities in adulthood. This can perpetuate cycles of poverty and inequality, as children who grow up in poverty are more likely to experience poverty as adults and pass it on to their own children.

However, it's important to remember that poverty is not an inherent characteristic of individuals or communities. Poverty is often the result of systemic inequalities and a lack of access to resources and opportunities. By addressing these root causes of poverty and providing individuals and communities with the resources and support they need to thrive, we can help break the cycle of poverty and create a more just and equitable society.

personal stories of individuals who have overcome poverty.

There are countless personal stories of individuals who have overcome poverty and achieved success, often through hard work, determination, and support from others. Here are just a few examples:

1. Oprah Winfrey - Born into poverty in rural Mississippi, Oprah Winfrey overcame a difficult childhood to become one of the most successful media moguls in the world. She has been open about her struggles with poverty, including wearing dresses made from potato sacks as a child. Despite these challenges, Winfrey worked hard in school and pursued a career in media, eventually landing her own talk show, which became a massive success.

2. J.K. Rowling - Before she became a best-selling author, J.K. Rowling was a struggling single mother living on welfare in Scotland. Despite her difficult circumstances, she continued to write and

eventually completed the first Harry Potter book, which went on to become a worldwide phenomenon. Today, Rowling is one of the wealthiest women in the world and a vocal advocate for social justice issues.

3. Les Brown - Born into poverty and abandoned by his mother at a young age, Les Brown faced numerous challenges throughout his childhood. Despite this, he refused to give up on his dreams of becoming a motivational speaker and pursued his goals with relentless determination. Today, Brown is a successful motivational speaker, author, and radio personality who has inspired millions of people around the world.

4. Tyler Perry - Tyler Perry is a successful filmmaker, actor, and producer who was once homeless and living in his car. He grew up in poverty in New Orleans and faced numerous challenges throughout his life, including abuse and homelessness. Despite these challenges, Perry continued to pursue his dreams of becoming a writer and eventually landed a deal to produce his first play. Today, he is a

successful filmmaker and entrepreneur, with a net worth of over $1 billion.

5. Richard Branson - Richard Branson is a British entrepreneur and founder of the Virgin Group. However, he didn't come from a wealthy background. He struggled in school and was diagnosed with dyslexia at a young age. Despite these challenges, Branson continued to pursue his dreams of starting his own business and eventually launched the Virgin Group, which includes more than 400 companies worldwide. Today, Branson is one of the wealthiest and most successful entrepreneurs in the world.

6. Chris Gardner - Chris Gardner is a successful businessman, author, and motivational speaker who overcame homelessness and poverty to achieve success. After struggling to make ends meet as a single father, Gardner landed an internship at a prestigious stock brokerage firm and eventually launched his own successful brokerage firm. Today, he is a successful businessman and author of the

book "The Pursuit of Happyness," which was turned into a successful movie starring Will Smith.

These personal stories are a testament to the resilience of the human spirit and the power of hard work and determination in the face of adversity. They remind us that, no matter how difficult our circumstances may be, we have the power to overcome them and achieve success. By sharing these stories and providing practical advice and support to individuals facing poverty, we can help inspire and empower others to achieve their own journey from rags to riches.

These personal stories also show that overcoming poverty is not easy, but it is possible with hard work, determination, and support. By sharing these stories and providing practical advice and support to individuals facing poverty, we can help inspire and empower others to achieve their own journey from rags to riches.

Strategies for overcoming poverty and building a foundation for success

Overcoming poverty requires a combination of hard work, determination, and strategic thinking. Here are some strategies that can help individuals build a foundation for success:

1. **Education** - Education is one of the most important tools for breaking the cycle of poverty. By investing in education and acquiring new skills, individuals can increase their earning potential and open up new opportunities for themselves. This can include pursuing formal education, such as a college degree or vocational training, or learning new skills through online courses or apprenticeships.

Education is often considered to be the great equalizer, providing individuals with the knowledge and skills they need to break free from the cycle of poverty. In many cases, the lack of access to quality education is what keeps people trapped in poverty. But education can also be the key that unlocks the door to a brighter future.

One of the most powerful ways to break the cycle of poverty is by investing in education. This can take many forms, from pursuing a college degree to learning a trade or skill through vocational training or apprenticeships. For many people, formal education is the key to unlocking new opportunities and higher earning potential.

But education doesn't always have to be formal. Online courses and self-directed learning can also provide valuable skills and knowledge that can help individuals advance in their careers and increase their earning potential. And for those who are struggling to make ends meet, even small investments in education can have a big impact, such as learning new financial skills or taking classes on job interview techniques.

By investing in education, individuals can gain the knowledge and skills they need to break free from the cycle of poverty and build a better life for themselves and their families. And when more people have access to quality education, it can have a ripple effect on entire communities, helping to lift people out of poverty and create a brighter future for everyone.

2. **Networking** - Building a strong network of contacts and mentors can be a valuable asset in overcoming poverty. By connecting with others in their industry or community, individuals can gain access to new opportunities and resources, as well as receive advice and support from others who have experienced similar challenges.

Networking is an essential skill for anyone looking to build wealth and overcome poverty. It involves making connections and building relationships with individuals who can offer support, guidance, and opportunities. Networking can take many forms, from attending industry events and conferences to reaching out to potential mentors or joining professional organizations.

One of the most significant benefits of networking is the access it provides to new opportunities. By connecting with individuals in their industry or community, individuals can learn about job openings, internships, and other career advancement opportunities that they might not have known about otherwise. Additionally, networking can help individuals develop new skills and knowledge by connecting with individuals who are experts in their field.

Another benefit of networking is the opportunity to receive advice and support from others who have experienced similar challenges. This can be particularly valuable for individuals who are trying to overcome poverty or build wealth, as they may be able to learn from the experiences of others who have been in their shoes. Mentors and peers can offer guidance on everything from career development to financial management, and can serve as a source of inspiration and motivation when times get tough.

Overall, networking is a critical tool for breaking the cycle of poverty and building a foundation for success. By investing time and effort into building strong relationships and connections, individuals can gain access to new opportunities, learn new skills, and receive advice and support from others who have overcome similar challenges.

3. **Entrepreneurship** - Starting a business or pursuing entrepreneurship can be a powerful way to build wealth and achieve financial independence. By identifying a need in their community or industry and developing a business plan, individuals can create their own opportunities and build a successful business.

Entrepreneurship is a path that allows individuals to take control of their financial destiny by creating their own opportunities. Starting a business requires an entrepreneurial mindset, which involves identifying gaps in the market and developing a unique solution to meet those needs. This requires creativity, problem-solving skills, and a willingness to take risks.

Entrepreneurship also provides a path to financial freedom that is not dependent on traditional employment. By building a successful business, individuals can generate passive income, which can provide a steady stream of revenue even when they are not actively working. This can give them the freedom to pursue other interests and enjoy a higher quality of life.

However, entrepreneurship is not without its challenges. Starting a business requires a significant investment of time, money, and resources. It also involves navigating complex legal and financial issues, as well as competing with established businesses in the market.

Despite these challenges, entrepreneurship can be a rewarding and fulfilling path for those who are willing to put in the work. By developing a strong business plan, building a solid team, and staying committed to their goals, individuals can create a successful business that provides financial stability and independence for themselves and their families.

4. **Financial management** - Effective financial management is key to building a strong foundation for success. This includes creating a budget, saving for emergencies and long-term goals, and avoiding debt and high-interest loans.

Effective financial management is a crucial skill that can help individuals overcome poverty and achieve financial freedom. By creating a budget and tracking their expenses, individuals can gain a better understanding of their financial situation and identify areas where they can cut costs or increase their income. They can also set financial goals and create a plan to achieve them, such as saving for a down payment on a house or paying off debt.

In addition, saving for emergencies and long-term goals is an important aspect of financial management. Having an emergency fund can provide a cushion in case of unexpected expenses, such as medical bills or car repairs, and prevent individuals from falling into debt. Investing in retirement accounts, such as a 401(k) or IRA, can also help individuals prepare for their future and achieve financial stability in their later years.

Furthermore, avoiding debt and high-interest loans is critical in building a strong financial foundation. High levels of debt can be overwhelming and make it difficult to achieve financial goals. It is important to understand the terms and conditions of any loans or credit cards before taking them on, and to only borrow what can be paid back in a timely manner.

In summary, effective financial management involves creating a budget, saving for emergencies and long-term goals, and avoiding debt and high-interest loans. By implementing these strategies, individuals can build a strong financial foundation and set themselves up for long-term success.

5. **Mentoring** - Finding a mentor or role model who has successfully overcome poverty can be a valuable source of inspiration and guidance. Mentors can provide advice, support, and guidance, as well as help individuals navigate the challenges of poverty.

Mentoring is an essential part of overcoming poverty, as it provides individuals with the opportunity to learn from someone who has successfully navigated similar challenges. A mentor can provide guidance, support, and encouragement to help individuals overcome obstacles and achieve their goals.

Mentoring relationships can take many forms, from informal connections with family members, friends, or community leaders, to more structured programs provided by non-profit organizations or professional associations. Regardless of the form it takes, a good mentoring relationship should be based on mutual trust and respect, with the mentor providing guidance and support while also allowing the mentee to take ownership of their own growth and development.

Mentors can offer a variety of benefits to those seeking to overcome poverty. They can provide advice on navigating the job market, building professional networks, and managing finances. They can also offer emotional support and encouragement, helping individuals to stay focused and motivated in the face of challenges and setbacks.

In addition to providing guidance and support, mentors can also serve as role models, showing individuals what is possible when they work hard and stay focused on their goals. By sharing their own stories of overcoming poverty, mentors can inspire and motivate others to pursue their own dreams and aspirations.

Overall, mentoring is a powerful tool for overcoming poverty and building a brighter future. By connecting with a mentor and building a strong mentoring relationship, individuals can gain the guidance, support, and inspiration they need to overcome obstacles and achieve their goals.

By combining these strategies and working hard to achieve their goals, individuals can overcome poverty and build a foundation for success. It's important to remember that overcoming poverty is a journey, and success may not come overnight. But with hard work, determination, and support, anyone can achieve their own journey from rags to riches.

6. **Building a support system** - Overcoming poverty can be a challenging and isolating experience, so building a strong support system is critical. This can include friends, family members, community organizations, or support groups. By surrounding themselves with positive and supportive people, individuals can gain the emotional and practical support they need to overcome poverty.

7. **Volunteerism and community service** - Giving back to the community through volunteer work and community service can be a powerful way to build connections, gain new skills, and make a positive impact. Volunteering can also provide opportunities to network with other like-minded individuals and

potentially open up new job or business opportunities.

8. **Developing a growth mindset** - Developing a growth mindset is crucial for overcoming poverty and achieving success. This means embracing challenges as opportunities for growth, learning from failure, and believing in the power of hard work and persistence.

Developing a growth mindset is all about adopting a positive attitude towards learning and personal development. People who have a growth mindset are more likely to view challenges as opportunities for growth, and they are more likely to embrace failure as a necessary step towards success.

In the context of overcoming poverty, developing a growth mindset can be especially important. Poverty can be a challenging and difficult situation to navigate, and it can be easy to fall into a cycle of hopelessness and despair. However, by cultivating a growth mindset, individuals can learn to view their situation as an opportunity for growth and change. They can become more resilient in the face of adversity, and they can learn to see setbacks as opportunities for learning and improvement.

Developing a growth mindset can involve a range of strategies, such as setting realistic goals, seeking out feedback and advice, and engaging in ongoing learning and development. It may also involve reframing negative self-talk and focusing on the positive aspects of one's situation.

Ultimately, developing a growth mindset is about recognizing that our abilities and potential are not fixed, but rather can be developed and improved over time. By embracing this mindset, individuals can overcome obstacles and achieve success in their personal and professional lives.

9. **Investing in health and wellness** - Investing in physical and mental health is important for building a strong foundation for success. This includes getting regular exercise, eating a healthy diet, getting

enough sleep, and seeking support for mental health challenges such as anxiety or depression.

10.   **Setting and achieving goals** - Setting and achieving goals is a key part of overcoming poverty and building a foundation for success. By setting specific, measurable, and achievable goals, individuals can track their progress and stay motivated as they work towards success.

By following these strategies and continuing to work hard towards their goals, individuals can overcome poverty and achieve their own journey from rags to riches. It takes time, effort, and perseverance, but with the right mindset and support, anything is possible.

Defining wealth and the different forms it can take

Wealth is often defined as an abundance of valuable resources or possessions. However, wealth can take many different forms beyond just material possessions or financial assets. Here are some examples of the different forms of wealth:

1. **Financial wealth** - This is the most commonly recognized form of wealth and refers to the accumulation of financial assets such as savings, investments, and property.

Financial wealth is the accumulation of financial assets, which can include cash, savings accounts, investment accounts, stocks, bonds, and real estate properties. It is the most commonly recognized form of wealth as it is tangible and can be easily quantified. The accumulation of financial wealth is often seen as a key indicator of success and can provide individuals with a sense of security and stability.

Financial wealth can be built through various means, such as investing in the stock market or real estate, saving and budgeting, and making sound financial decisions. It can also be inherited or acquired through other means, such as receiving a large settlement or winning the lottery.

However, it is important to note that financial wealth alone does not necessarily guarantee happiness or fulfillment. It is important to also consider other forms of wealth, such as social and emotional wealth, in order to achieve overall well-being and satisfaction in life.

2. **wealth Physical** - Physical wealth refers to the tangible possessions that individuals own, such as cars, houses, and jewelry.

Physical wealth includes all tangible assets that individuals possess, such as real estate, vehicles, jewelry, and other personal belongings. This type of wealth is often viewed as a symbol of success and status, and it can provide individuals with a sense of security and stability. However, physical wealth is also subject to external factors such as market fluctuations and natural disasters, making it important for individuals to manage and protect their physical assets.

In some cases, physical wealth may also include a person's health and well-being. This can be considered a form of physical wealth because it is an asset that individuals can invest in and maintain, and it can have a significant impact on their quality of life and ability to pursue their goals.

While physical wealth can provide individuals with a sense of comfort and security, it is important to remember that true wealth extends beyond material possessions. Developing strong relationships, pursuing personal growth and fulfillment, and making a positive impact in the world are all essential components of a truly wealthy life.

3. **Intellectual wealth** - Intellectual wealth refers to the knowledge, skills, and expertise that individuals possess. This can include formal education, training, and experience in a particular field.
   Intellectual wealth is an essential aspect of an

individual's overall wealth. It encompasses the knowledge, skills, and expertise that an individual has gained over time through various learning experiences. Intellectual wealth is not limited to formal education, although formal education can be an excellent way to acquire knowledge and skills in a specific field.

Intellectual wealth can also be acquired through self-education, reading books, attending workshops, and gaining experience through practical work. The more knowledge and skills an individual possesses, the more they are likely to be successful in their personal and professional life. For instance, having advanced skills in a particular field can increase an individual's chances of being hired by top companies or even starting their own business.

Moreover, intellectual wealth can provide individuals with a competitive advantage in their respective fields, allowing them to innovate, create, and come up with new ideas. It can also enable them to adapt to changing circumstances and think critically about problems they encounter, leading to more effective solutions.

In summary, intellectual wealth is an essential aspect of an individual's overall wealth. It is not just about formal education but also encompasses the skills, knowledge, and expertise gained through various learning experiences. It can open doors to new opportunities, improve employability, and provide a competitive advantage in a rapidly changing world.

4. **Emotional wealth** - Emotional wealth refers to the quality of an individual's relationships and their ability to experience positive emotions such as love, joy, and contentment.

Emotional wealth is a form of wealth that is often overlooked, but it is just as important as the other forms of wealth. Emotional wealth is about the quality of one's relationships, including their ability to form deep, meaningful connections with others. It also includes their ability to manage their emotions and experience positive feelings such as love, joy, and contentment.

Having emotional wealth can provide a sense of security and stability, which can help individuals overcome challenges and adversity. It can also provide a strong support system during difficult times, as well as a sense of purpose and fulfillment in life.

One way to develop emotional wealth is to cultivate positive relationships with friends, family, and colleagues. This can be achieved by being a good listener, showing empathy and understanding, and being open and honest in communication.

Another important aspect of emotional wealth is the ability to manage one's emotions effectively. This involves developing emotional intelligence, which includes recognizing and managing one's own emotions, as well as understanding and responding to the emotions of others. Emotional intelligence can be developed through self-reflection, mindfulness practices, and seeking feedback from others.

In summary, emotional wealth is an essential form of wealth that can provide individuals with a sense of security, stability, and fulfillment. It can be developed by cultivating positive relationships and developing emotional intelligence. By focusing on developing emotional wealth in addition to other forms of wealth, individuals can achieve a more well-rounded and fulfilling life.

5. **Spiritual wealth** - Spiritual wealth refers to an individual's sense of purpose, meaning, and connection to a higher power or belief system.

Spiritual wealth goes beyond the material possessions and encompasses the inner sense of fulfillment and contentment. It relates to the search for deeper meaning and purpose in life, and a connection to a higher power or belief system. For some, spiritual wealth may come from practicing a particular religion, while for others, it may involve pursuing a personal spiritual practice or philosophy.

Individuals who possess spiritual wealth often report feeling a sense of inner peace and fulfillment, even in the face of challenging circumstances. They may also be more resilient and able to navigate difficult situations with greater ease. In addition, spiritual wealth can provide individuals with a sense of perspective and help them to prioritize their values and goals in life.

Developing spiritual wealth can involve engaging in activities such as meditation, prayer, or participating in a spiritual community. It may also involve exploring personal beliefs and values, and seeking a deeper understanding of one's place in the world. By cultivating spiritual wealth, individuals can experience a greater sense of purpose and meaning in life, and find fulfillment beyond material possessions.

6. **Cultural wealth** - Cultural wealth refers to an individual's connection to their cultural identity, heritage, and traditions.

Cultural wealth is an often-overlooked form of wealth that is crucial for individuals to have a sense of identity and belonging. It encompasses the customs, beliefs, practices, and values of a particular community, whether that community is based on ethnicity, religion, language, or other shared characteristics.

Having a strong connection to one's cultural identity can provide a sense of pride, belonging, and connection to a larger community. It can also help individuals navigate the challenges of living in a society that may not always embrace or celebrate their cultural background.

Cultural wealth can also provide individuals with a unique perspective and skillset that can be valuable in a globalized economy. For example, being bilingual or having experience with different cultural practices can be a valuable asset in fields such as international business, diplomacy, or social work.

In addition, cultural wealth can serve as a source of creativity and innovation, as individuals draw on their unique experiences and perspectives to create new ideas and solutions to complex problems.

Overall, cultural wealth is a vital form of wealth that should be celebrated and embraced as a valuable asset in individuals and communities.

7. **Social wealth** - Social wealth refers to an individual's social connections and support systems, including their family, friends, and community.

Social wealth refers to an individual's ability to form and maintain healthy relationships with others. It is a measure of the quality and depth of an individual's social connections, including their family, friends, and community. A strong social network can provide emotional support, practical assistance, and access to resources and opportunities that can help individuals overcome poverty and achieve success. Social wealth can also include an individual's participation in social organizations and groups, as well as their engagement with their community and society at large. By investing in their social connections and contributing to their community, individuals can build social wealth that can serve as a foundation for a successful and fulfilling life.

It's important to recognize that wealth can take many different forms beyond just financial assets or material possessions. By focusing on developing a variety of forms of wealth, individuals can lead fulfilling and well-rounded lives that are rich in experiences, relationships, and personal growth.

8. **Time wealth** - Time is a valuable resource that cannot be replenished once it is spent. Time wealth refers to an individual's ability to control their own

time and use it in ways that align with their values and priorities. This can include having flexibility in work schedules, having enough free time for hobbies and leisure activities, and being able to spend time with loved ones.

Time wealth is all about having control over your time and being able to use it in ways that are important to you. It's not just about having free time or a flexible work schedule, but it's also about being able to prioritize your time based on your values and goals. Individuals who have time wealth are able to balance their work and personal lives, and they have the freedom to pursue their passions and interests.

One key aspect of time wealth is the ability to manage time effectively. This involves setting clear priorities, setting goals and deadlines, and avoiding distractions and time-wasting activities. Individuals who are skilled in time management are able to maximize their productivity and make the most of their time.

Another important component of time wealth is having a sense of control over one's time. This means being able to choose how to spend one's time and having the freedom to make decisions about work and personal commitments. Individuals who feel in control of their time are less likely to experience stress and burnout, and they are more likely to feel satisfied with their lives.

Time wealth is not just about having more time, but it's about using the time we have in a way that aligns with our values and priorities. It's about making intentional choices and being present in the moment. By developing time wealth, individuals can achieve a sense of fulfillment and purpose in their lives.

9. **Environmental wealth** - Environmental wealth refers to an individual's access to clean air, water, and natural resources. It also includes the ability to live in a safe and healthy environment that is free from pollution and environmental hazards.

10. **Health wealth** - Health is an essential form of wealth that enables individuals to live long, happy, and productive lives. This includes physical health, mental health, and emotional well-being.

Health wealth is a form of wealth that is often overlooked but is crucial for overall well-being and happiness. Physical health refers to the state of a person's body and their ability to perform daily tasks and activities without limitations. This can include maintaining a healthy diet, exercising regularly, and getting enough sleep. Mental health refers to a person's psychological well-being, including their ability to cope with stress, manage emotions, and maintain a positive outlook on life. Emotional well-being refers to a person's ability to experience positive emotions, such as happiness and contentment, and to manage negative emotions, such as anxiety and depression.

Investing in health wealth can have a positive impact on all other forms of wealth, as it enables individuals to live longer, be more productive, and enjoy their lives to the fullest. This can include investing in preventative measures such as regular medical check-ups, practicing stress-reducing activities such as meditation or yoga, and seeking professional help for mental health or emotional issues when necessary. In addition, building a support system of family, friends, and healthcare professionals can also contribute to a person's overall health wealth. By prioritizing and investing in health wealth, individuals can enjoy a higher quality of life and be better equipped to pursue their other forms of wealth.

11. **Creative wealth** - Creative wealth refers to an individual's ability to express themselves creatively and to generate new ideas and solutions. This can include artistic talent, innovative thinking, and problem-solving skills.

By understanding the different forms of wealth, individuals can broaden their definition of success and focus on building a well-rounded and fulfilling life. Wealth is not just about accumulating money or possessions, but also about developing strong relationships, pursuing personal growth, and contributing to the world in meaningful ways.

Personal stories of individuals who have built wealth

There are countless stories of individuals who have gone from rags to riches and built wealth in a variety of different ways. Here are a few examples of individuals who have built wealth through their own hard work, perseverance, and ingenuity:

1. Oprah Winfrey - Oprah Winfrey is one of the most successful and influential media personalities of our time. Despite being born into poverty in rural Mississippi, she worked hard to overcome the challenges she faced and eventually built a media empire that includes a television network, a magazine, and a variety of other successful ventures.

2. Warren Buffett - Warren Buffett is one of the most successful investors of all time. He grew up in modest circumstances in Nebraska and began his career as a stockbroker. Through years of disciplined

investing and careful analysis, he built a fortune that now exceeds $100 billion.

3. J.K. Rowling - J.K. Rowling is the author of the wildly successful Harry Potter book series. Before she became a household name, however, she was a struggling single mother living on welfare in Edinburgh, Scotland. Despite numerous rejections from publishers, she persisted in pursuing her dream of becoming a writer and eventually found success beyond her wildest dreams.

4. Sara Blakely - Sara Blakely is the founder of Spanx, a wildly successful company that produces slimming undergarments for women. Blakely grew up in a modest household in Florida and worked a variety of odd jobs before coming up with the idea for Spanx. Through sheer determination and hard work, she built the company into a multi-billion dollar enterprise.

5. Elon Musk - Elon Musk is a serial entrepreneur and the founder of a variety of successful companies, including Tesla, SpaceX, and PayPal. Despite growing up in difficult circumstances in South Africa, Musk

was able to turn his intelligence and vision into an incredible level of success.

These are just a few examples of individuals who have built wealth through their own hard work, ingenuity, and perseverance. By studying their stories, we can learn valuable lessons about what it takes to build wealth and achieve success in life.

more

6. Steve Jobs - Steve Jobs is the co-founder of Apple, one of the most successful and innovative companies in the world. Despite being adopted and dropping out of college, Jobs went on to build a career that revolutionized the technology industry and changed the way we interact with computers and other devices.

7. Richard Branson - Richard Branson is a serial entrepreneur and the founder of Virgin Group, a conglomerate that includes over 400 companies in a variety of different industries. Despite struggling with dyslexia as a child and dropping out of school at

a young age, Branson was able to turn his natural charisma and entrepreneurial spirit into incredible success.

8. Jay-Z - Jay-Z is one of the most successful and influential rappers of all time. Born into poverty in Brooklyn, New York, he hustled his way to the top of the music industry through hard work, talent, and a relentless drive to succeed. In addition to his music career, he has built a successful business empire that includes record labels, fashion lines, and other ventures.

9. Jack Ma - Jack Ma is the founder of Alibaba, one of the largest e-commerce companies in the world. Despite growing up in poverty in China and facing numerous rejections before launching Alibaba, Ma was able to build a successful business through a combination of hard work, creativity, and an unwavering belief in his vision.

10. Mark Cuban - Mark Cuban is a billionaire entrepreneur and investor who has founded numerous successful companies and invested in many others. Despite growing up in a working-class

family in Pittsburgh, Pennsylvania, Cuban was able to achieve incredible success through his intelligence, hard work, and willingness to take risks.

These personal stories of individuals who have built wealth demonstrate that success can come in many different forms and from many different paths. By studying their stories and learning from their experiences, we can gain valuable insights into what it takes to achieve wealth and success in our own lives.

Strategies for building wealth through entrepreneurship, investing, and saving

Building wealth can be a complex process, but there are several strategies that have proven to be effective for many successful entrepreneurs and investors. Here are some key strategies for building wealth:

1. **Entrepreneurship** - Starting a business can be a powerful way to build wealth. By identifying a need in the market and creating a product or service to fill that need, entrepreneurs can generate significant revenue and build value in their companies. Successful entrepreneurs also tend to be creative, hardworking, and willing to take risks in order to achieve their goals.

2. **Investing** - Investing can be another powerful way to build wealth over time. By investing in stocks, real estate, or other assets, investors can benefit from compound interest and capital gains over the long term. Successful investors tend to be patient,

disciplined, and knowledgeable about the markets they invest in.

3. **Saving** - Building wealth also requires saving money over time. By living below your means and putting money aside in savings accounts, retirement funds, or other investment vehicles, you can accumulate wealth and build a strong financial foundation for the future.

4. **Diversification** - Successful wealth building also requires diversification across different asset classes and investment vehicles. By spreading your risk across different types of assets, you can reduce your exposure to any one particular investment and protect your wealth over the long term.

5. **Education** - Finally, building wealth requires ongoing education and learning. By staying up-to-date with market trends, financial news, and investment strategies, you can make informed decisions about how to grow your wealth over time.

By incorporating these strategies into your financial plan, you can build wealth over time and achieve your financial goals. Whether you are starting a business, investing in the stock market, or saving for retirement, the key is to be disciplined, patient, and persistent in your efforts.

To dive deeper into these strategies, let's explore each one in more detail:

1. **Entrepreneurship** - Starting a business can be a powerful way to build wealth because it allows you to create a product or service that solves a problem in the market. Successful entrepreneurs are often passionate about their work and are driven to succeed. They are also willing to take risks and work hard to build their businesses. However, entrepreneurship also requires a significant amount of time, effort, and capital to get started. It's important to do your research and create a solid business plan before taking the leap.

2. **Investing** - Investing can be a powerful way to build wealth over the long term. By investing in stocks, real estate, or other assets, you can benefit from compound interest and capital gains. However,

investing also requires discipline and patience. It's important to develop a long-term investment strategy and stick to it, even when the markets are volatile. It's also important to diversify your investments across different asset classes and industries to reduce your risk.

3. **Saving** - Building wealth also requires saving money over time. By living below your means and putting money aside in savings accounts, retirement funds, or other investment vehicles, you can accumulate wealth and build a strong financial foundation for the future. However, saving also requires discipline and sacrifice. It's important to prioritize your spending and make sure that you are putting enough money aside for your long-term financial goals.

4. **Diversification -** Successful wealth building also requires diversification across different asset classes and investment vehicles. By spreading your risk across different types of assets, you can reduce your exposure to any one particular investment and protect your wealth over the long term. However, diversification also requires research and due

diligence. It's important to understand the risks and potential returns of each investment before making a decision.

5. **Education** - Finally, building wealth requires ongoing education and learning. By staying up-to-date with market trends, financial news, and investment strategies, you can make informed decisions about how to grow your wealth over time. However, education also requires time and effort. It's important to stay curious and open-minded, and to seek out resources and mentors who can help you on your journey.

By incorporating these strategies into your financial plan, you can build wealth over time and achieve your financial goals. Remember, building wealth is a marathon, not a sprint. It requires patience, discipline, and persistence. But with the right mindset and strategies, anyone can achieve financial success and create a better life for themselves and their families.

Common challenges faced by individuals seeking wealth

While building wealth is a worthwhile goal, it's not without its challenges. Here are some common obstacles that individuals may face when seeking to build wealth:

1. **Lack of financial education** - Many people do not have a strong foundation in personal finance or investment strategies. Without this knowledge, they may struggle to make informed decisions about their money and investments.

Lack of financial education is a common barrier that prevents individuals from achieving financial wealth. Many people lack the necessary knowledge and skills to effectively manage their finances, make wise investments, and build wealth over time. This can result in poor financial decisions, such as overspending, taking on too much debt, or failing to save for the future.

Furthermore, the lack of financial education can lead to individuals being vulnerable to scams and fraudulent activities. They may fall victim to high-interest loans, fraudulent investments, or other financial schemes that promise quick riches but ultimately leave them in a worse financial situation.

Without a strong foundation in financial education, individuals may not fully understand the importance of budgeting, saving, and investing. They may miss out on opportunities to grow their wealth over time and secure their financial future. Overall, a lack of financial education can be a significant obstacle to building financial wealth and achieving long-term financial success.

2. **Debt** - Debt can be a significant obstacle to building wealth. High-interest debt, such as credit card debt, can quickly accumulate and eat away at your savings. It's important to prioritize paying off debt before focusing on building wealth.

Debt can be a major obstacle to building wealth and achieving financial security. Many people carry significant amounts of debt, whether it's from student loans, credit cards, or other forms of borrowing. High-interest debt, such as credit card debt, can quickly accumulate and eat away at your savings, making it difficult to build wealth.

Debt can also affect an individual's credit score, which is a crucial factor in securing loans and credit. A poor credit score can result in higher interest rates on loans and credit cards, further compounding the debt problem.

To overcome the obstacle of debt, it's important to prioritize paying it off as soon as possible. This may involve creating a budget and cutting unnecessary expenses to free up money to put towards debt repayment. It may also involve negotiating with creditors to reduce interest rates or creating a debt repayment plan.

By tackling debt head-on, individuals can take control of their financial situation and pave the way for building wealth in the future.

3. **Lack of discipline** - Building wealth requires discipline and a long-term perspective. Without this mindset, it can be easy to give in to short-term impulses and spend money on things that don't contribute to your long-term financial goals.

Lack of discipline is a significant challenge to building wealth. It takes discipline to consistently save money, invest wisely, and make responsible financial decisions. Unfortunately, many individuals lack the discipline needed to build and maintain their wealth. They may struggle to control their spending, fall prey to impulsive purchases, or fail to prioritize their long-term financial goals.

Without discipline, it can be easy to give in to temptations and overspend, especially when faced with unexpected expenses or emergencies. This can lead to accumulating debt, which can significantly impede one's ability to build wealth over time. Additionally, lacking discipline can result in missed opportunities for investment or saving.

To overcome this challenge, it is crucial to develop a disciplined approach to managing one's finances. This includes creating a budget, sticking to a savings plan, and avoiding unnecessary expenses. It also involves building the mental fortitude to resist short-term temptations and stay focused on long-term financial goals. By developing discipline and staying committed to their financial plan, individuals can gradually build wealth and achieve financial stability.

4. **Fear and risk aversion** - Building wealth often requires taking risks, such as starting a business or investing in the stock market. For some individuals, this can be scary or overwhelming. It's important to understand and manage your risk tolerance, but also to be willing to take calculated risks in order to achieve your financial goals.

Fear and risk aversion can be significant obstacles to building wealth. Many individuals are hesitant to take risks or make investments due to a fear of failure, loss, or uncertainty. However, avoiding risk altogether can also mean missing out on potential opportunities for growth and financial gain.

It's important to understand and manage your risk tolerance, which is the level of risk you are comfortable taking on. This can depend on factors such as your financial situation, age, and personal goals. For example, a younger person with a stable income and few financial obligations may be more willing to take on higher-risk investments than someone closer to retirement.

At the same time, it's crucial to take calculated risks that align with your financial goals and values. This means doing your research, seeking out advice from trusted sources, and making informed decisions based on your individual circumstances.

By learning to manage fear and risk aversion, individuals can open themselves up to new opportunities for wealth-building, such as starting a business, investing in stocks or real estate, or pursuing higher education or professional development. It's important to remember that building wealth requires a long-term perspective and a willingness to take risks in pursuit of your goals.

5. **Lack of access to resources** - Building wealth often requires access to resources such as capital, mentorship, and professional advice. For individuals who do not have access to these resources, it can be challenging to get started or make progress.

Expanding on the point of lack of access to resources, building wealth requires access to a range of resources and support systems that can help individuals overcome obstacles and achieve their financial goals. However, not everyone has equal access to these resources. For example, individuals living in underprivileged areas or with limited financial means may not have access to capital or investment opportunities that could help them build wealth. They may also lack access to networks of successful business owners or financial advisors who can provide guidance and support.

Additionally, some groups may face systemic barriers to accessing resources, such as discrimination based on race, gender, or socioeconomic status. These barriers can make it difficult for individuals to access resources such as business loans or investment opportunities, even if they have the skills and knowledge to succeed. This lack of access can further perpetuate the wealth gap and contribute to the cycle of poverty.

Therefore, it is essential to work towards creating more equitable access to resources and support systems that can help individuals build wealth, regardless of their background or circumstances. This can include initiatives such as increasing funding for small business loans, providing mentorship and training programs, and creating policies that promote financial education and literacy. By improving access to resources, more individuals can overcome the challenges of poverty and achieve financial success.

By understanding and addressing these challenges, individuals can develop strategies to overcome them and build wealth over time. Whether it's through education, debt reduction, discipline, risk management, or resource acquisition, there are ways to navigate these obstacles and achieve financial success.

6. Systemic barriers - For some individuals, systemic barriers such as discrimination, lack of access to

education, or a limited social network can make it more difficult to build wealth. These barriers may require systemic solutions, such as policy changes or community support programs, to help level the playing field.

7. **Life events** - Life events such as job loss, health issues, or unexpected expenses can disrupt financial plans and make it more difficult to build wealth. It's important to have contingency plans in place and to be flexible in adjusting your financial goals as circumstances change.

8. **Lack of motivation** - Building wealth can be a long-term goal, and it can be challenging to stay motivated over time. It's important to identify your reasons for wanting to build wealth and to remind yourself of these reasons regularly.

9. **Comparison with others** - Comparing your financial situation to others can be demotivating and distracting. It's important to focus on your own goals and progress, rather than comparing yourself to others.

10. **Mindset and self-limiting beliefs** - Your mindset and beliefs about money can play a significant role in your ability to build wealth. Negative self-talk or limiting beliefs can hold you back from taking risks or pursuing opportunities. It's important to work on developing a positive, growth-oriented mindset in order to achieve financial success.

By understanding and addressing these common challenges, individuals can develop strategies to overcome them and build a strong foundation for wealth building. It's important to be patient, persistent, and proactive in pursuing your financial goals. With the right mindset and approach, anyone can achieve financial success and create a better future for themselves and their families.

Strategies for overcoming these challenges, such as mindset, resilience, and persistence

To overcome the challenges faced in building wealth, it's important to adopt a mindset of growth, resilience, and persistence. Here are some strategies to help:

1. **Mindset** - Develop a growth mindset, which sees challenges as opportunities to learn and grow. Focus on your strengths and skills, and cultivate a positive attitude toward money and wealth.

Developing a growth mindset is crucial for building wealth and achieving financial success. A growth mindset is the belief that your abilities and intelligence can be developed through hard work, dedication, and learning. This mindset encourages individuals to embrace challenges as opportunities for growth and learning, rather than as threats or obstacles.

To cultivate a growth mindset, it's important to focus on your strengths and skills, and to believe in your ability to learn and grow. This means being willing to take risks, try new things, and embrace failure as a learning opportunity. It's also important to surround yourself with positive influences, such as mentors or role models who have successfully built wealth and achieved financial success.

In addition to developing a growth mindset, it's important to cultivate a positive attitude toward money and wealth. This means recognizing the value of money and the role it plays in achieving your goals, while also understanding that money is a tool, not an end in itself. It's also important to develop healthy financial habits, such as budgeting, saving, and investing, in order to build a strong foundation for long-term financial success.

Overall, developing a growth mindset and a positive attitude toward money and wealth can help individuals overcome obstacles and achieve their financial goals. By embracing challenges as opportunities for growth and learning, and by cultivating healthy financial habits, individuals can build a strong foundation for long-term financial success.

2. **Resilience** - Develop resilience by practicing self-care, building a support network, and maintaining a sense of purpose and meaning. This can help you bounce back from setbacks and stay motivated in pursuing your financial goals.

Expanding on resilience, it is the ability to bounce back from adversity, overcome obstacles, and thrive in the face of challenges. It's important to cultivate resilience when pursuing financial goals because setbacks and failures are inevitable. Resilience can be developed by practicing self-care, such as getting enough sleep, eating well, and exercising regularly. These habits can help you manage stress and maintain a positive attitude.

Building a support network is also important for resilience. Surround yourself with people who support your goals and believe in your abilities. These individuals can provide emotional support and help you stay motivated during difficult times.

In addition, maintaining a sense of purpose and meaning can help build resilience. Focus on why you are pursuing financial goals and what they mean to you. This can help you stay focused and motivated, even when faced with setbacks.

Overall, developing resilience is crucial when pursuing financial goals. It can help you overcome obstacles, stay motivated, and ultimately achieve success.

3. **Persistence** - Develop persistence by setting specific, measurable goals, breaking them down into manageable steps, and tracking your progress. Celebrate small wins along the way to stay motivated and build momentum.

Persistence is a key factor in building wealth and achieving financial success. Developing persistence requires setting specific and measurable goals, breaking them down into manageable steps, and tracking your progress along the way. By doing so, you can gain a clear sense of direction and purpose and stay motivated even when faced with setbacks or obstacles.

To develop persistence, it's important to establish realistic goals that align with your values and priorities. These goals should be specific and measurable, with clear deadlines and milestones to help you stay on track. Once you've established your goals, break them down into smaller, more manageable steps. This can help you avoid feeling overwhelmed and make progress toward your goals more quickly.

It's also important to celebrate small wins along the way. This can help you stay motivated and build momentum toward your larger goals. Celebrating your progress can also help you develop a sense of accomplishment and pride in your achievements.

In addition to setting goals and tracking your progress, it's important to maintain a positive attitude and a growth mindset. This means seeing setbacks and challenges as opportunities to learn and grow, rather than as failures. It also means focusing on your strengths and skills, and cultivating a sense of optimism and hope for the future.

Finally, building persistence requires consistency and commitment. It's important to stay focused on your goals, even when faced with distractions or competing priorities. This may require making sacrifices or adjustments in other areas of your life, such as cutting back on unnecessary expenses or dedicating more time and energy to your financial goals. By maintaining a strong sense of purpose and staying committed to your goals, you can build the persistence and resilience needed to achieve financial success.

4. **Education** - Invest in education to increase your skills, knowledge, and opportunities. This can include formal education, training programs, or self-directed learning.

Investing in education is a powerful way to increase your earning potential, expand your knowledge, and improve your overall financial situation. Formal education, such as obtaining a degree or certification, can open up new job opportunities and help you command higher salaries. However, education can also take on many other forms, such as attending workshops, taking online courses, or participating in mentorship programs.

Self-directed learning can be an excellent way to expand your knowledge and skills, especially if you have limited financial resources or are unable to attend formal education programs. There are numerous resources available online, such as free courses, tutorials, and e-books that cover a range of topics from personal finance to entrepreneurship. Participating in online communities, attending webinars, and listening to podcasts can also be a great way to learn from others and stay up to date on current trends and best practices.

Investing in education can also help you stay competitive in today's rapidly changing job market. As technology continues to transform the way we work, staying current with the latest skills and knowledge is essential. By continually investing in your education, you can remain relevant and marketable to potential employers and clients.

In summary, investing in education can be a powerful tool for building wealth and achieving financial success. Whether through formal education or self-directed learning, it is an investment in yourself that can pay dividends for years to come.

5. **Community** - Build a supportive community of like-minded individuals who can provide advice, encouragement, and accountability. This can include family, friends, mentors, or professional networks.

Building a supportive community is an important step in achieving financial success. By surrounding yourself with like-minded individuals who share your goals and values, you can gain valuable advice, encouragement, and accountability.

One way to build a community is to seek out like-minded individuals in your personal and professional life. This could involve attending networking events, joining a professional association or group, or participating in online communities or forums. By connecting with others who are also pursuing financial success, you can learn from their experiences and benefit from their support.

Another way to build a community is to seek out mentorship from individuals who have achieved financial success. This could involve seeking out a financial advisor, joining a mentorship program, or simply reaching out to successful individuals in your network. By learning from the experiences of others who have achieved financial success, you can gain valuable insights and guidance for your own journey.

In addition to seeking out a supportive community, it's also important to contribute to the community and give back. This can involve volunteering or supporting causes that align with your values, or simply sharing your own experiences and advice with others who may be on a similar journey. By contributing to the community, you can strengthen your own sense of purpose and motivation, while also building relationships and connections that can be valuable in achieving your financial goals.

By adopting these strategies and building a strong foundation of mindset, resilience, and persistence, individuals can overcome the challenges of building wealth and achieve their financial goals. It's important to remember that building wealth is a long-term process that requires patience, discipline, and dedication. However, with the right approach and mindset, anyone can create a brighter financial future for themselves and their families.

Other strategies that can help individuals overcome challenges in building wealth include:

1. **Budgeting** - Creating and sticking to a budget can help individuals manage their expenses, reduce debt, and increase savings. It's important to prioritize essential expenses and minimize unnecessary spending.

2. **Investing** - Investing in stocks, real estate, or other assets can help individuals grow their wealth over time. It's important to research and diversify investments to manage risk and maximize returns.

3. **Entrepreneurship** - Starting a business can provide individuals with greater control over their income and financial future. It's important to develop a solid business plan, seek mentorship and support, and manage risks effectively.

4. **Financial literacy** - Building financial literacy skills can help individuals make informed decisions about their money, investments, and debt. It's important

to learn about personal finance, taxes, and retirement planning.

5. **Networking** - Building a professional network can provide individuals with access to opportunities, resources, and advice. It's important to attend networking events, build relationships, and offer value to others.

6. **Taking calculated risks** - While it's important to manage risks effectively, taking calculated risks can also provide opportunities for growth and financial gain. This can include investing in stocks or real estate, starting a business, or pursuing higher education or professional certifications.

7. **Creating multiple income streams** - Diversifying income streams can provide individuals with greater stability and flexibility. This can include starting a side business, freelancing, investing in stocks or real estate, or renting out a property.

8. **Minimizing debt** - Minimizing debt and managing it effectively can help individuals build wealth by reducing interest payments and freeing up cash flow.

This can include paying off high-interest debt first, consolidating debt, and negotiating payment terms.

9. **Seeking professional advice** - Seeking professional advice from financial advisors, accountants, or attorneys can help individuals make informed decisions about their money and investments. It's important to research and choose qualified professionals who have experience and expertise in relevant areas.

10. **Giving back** - Giving back to the community can provide individuals with a sense of purpose and fulfillment, while also building their personal brand and network. This can include volunteering, donating to charitable causes, or mentoring others.

By adopting these strategies and continuing to learn and grow, individuals can overcome challenges and build wealth over time. It's important to stay focused on long-term goals and be patient and persistent in pursuing them. Building wealth is a journey, and with the right mindset, skills, and strategies, anyone can achieve financial success.

Overall, building wealth requires a combination of mindset, skills, and strategies. By adopting a growth mindset, developing resilience and persistence, and implementing effective financial strategies, individuals can overcome challenges and build a strong foundation for long-term financial success.

Defining financial freedom and what it means to different individuals

Financial freedom is the ability to live the life you want without being constrained by financial worries or obligations. For some, it means having enough money to travel the world, retire early, or pursue their passions without worrying about making ends meet. For others, it means having enough money to support their families, pay off debt, or save for the future.

The concept of financial freedom is different for everyone, and it depends on factors such as lifestyle choices, personal values, and financial goals. However, some common characteristics of financial freedom include:

1. **Having a stable source of income that is sufficient to meet one's needs and wants.**

Having a stable source of income that is sufficient to meet one's needs and wants is a fundamental aspect of building wealth. A stable source of income can provide a sense of security and stability, which can in turn support financial planning and decision-making. It allows individuals to meet their basic needs, such as housing, food, and healthcare, and also gives them the ability to pursue their goals and aspirations.

Having a sufficient income also means having the ability to save and invest money for the future. This can be done through setting up a budget and saving a portion of one's income regularly. Building wealth requires discipline and a long-term perspective, and having a stable source of income can provide the foundation for this.

Additionally, a stable source of income can also provide opportunities for personal and professional growth. It can allow individuals to pursue further education or training, develop new skills, and take on new challenges. This can increase their earning potential and further support their financial goals.

However, it's important to note that a stable source of income alone may not be enough to build long-term wealth. It also requires managing expenses and making wise financial decisions.

2. Being debt-free or managing debt effectively.

Being debt-free or managing debt effectively is an important aspect of building wealth. High levels of debt can be a significant obstacle to achieving financial security and can eat away at your income and savings. It's important to prioritize paying off debt, especially high-interest debt like credit card debt, before focusing on building wealth.

Managing debt effectively means taking steps to reduce your debt load and make timely payments to creditors. This can include creating a budget and sticking to it, negotiating with creditors to lower interest rates or payment terms, and exploring options like consolidation or refinancing.

By being debt-free or managing debt effectively, you can free up more of your income for saving and investing, which can help you build wealth over time. It also gives you a sense of financial freedom and peace of mind, knowing that you are in control of your finances and not burdened by debt.

3. Having a solid savings and investment plan that provides financial security and growth.

Having a solid savings and investment plan is crucial for achieving financial security and growth. Savings are a fundamental aspect of financial planning, as they provide a safety net for unexpected expenses and emergencies. It's recommended to have an emergency fund that can cover at least three to six months of living expenses.

In addition to savings, investing can be an effective way to grow your wealth over time. Investing allows your money to work for you, earning returns that can help you achieve your financial goals. It's important to have a well-diversified investment portfolio that balances risk and return according to your investment objectives and risk tolerance.

To create a solid savings and investment plan, you should start by setting specific financial goals and developing a plan to achieve them. This may involve working with a financial advisor to develop a personalized investment strategy that aligns with your goals and risk tolerance. It's also important to regularly review and adjust your plan as needed to ensure that you stay on track toward achieving your financial goals.

4. Having the ability to make choices and pursue opportunities without being constrained by financial concerns.

Having financial freedom is a crucial aspect of wealth that allows individuals to make choices based on their desires and aspirations, rather than being limited by financial constraints. This could mean pursuing a career change, starting a business, traveling, or pursuing a passion project without worrying about the financial implications.

Achieving financial freedom requires careful planning and discipline. It involves creating a solid financial plan, which includes setting clear financial goals and creating a budget that supports those goals. This also means living below one's means and avoiding unnecessary expenses that do not align with one's long-term financial objectives.

One important step in achieving financial freedom is to build an emergency fund that can cover unexpected expenses or income loss. This fund can help individuals avoid taking on debt in times of crisis, which can set them back financially.

In addition to saving and investing, having a diversified portfolio of assets can also provide financial security and growth. This may include stocks, real estate, and other investment vehicles that align with one's risk tolerance and financial goals.

Overall, having financial freedom provides individuals with the ability to pursue their dreams and aspirations without being limited by financial constraints. It requires careful planning, discipline, and a long-term perspective, but the rewards can be significant in terms of personal fulfillment and achievement.

5. Living a life that is in alignment with one's values and priorities.

Living a life that is in alignment with one's values and priorities means having a clear understanding of what is most important to you and making choices that reflect those values. This can include things like spending time with loved ones, pursuing meaningful work, giving back to your community, or prioritizing self-care.

When you live in alignment with your values and priorities, you are more likely to feel fulfilled and satisfied with your life. This can also help you make better financial decisions, as you are more likely to prioritize spending on things that truly matter to you.

To live a life in alignment with your values and priorities, it's important to take the time to reflect on what matters most to you. This may involve asking yourself questions like: What do I value most in life? What are my top priorities? What brings me the most joy and fulfillment?

Once you have a clear understanding of your values and priorities, you can then make intentional choices about how you spend your time and money. This may involve setting boundaries, saying no to things that don't align with your values, or seeking out opportunities that do align with your priorities.

Living a life in alignment with your values and priorities is an ongoing process that requires reflection and self-awareness. However, it can lead to a greater sense of purpose, fulfillment, and financial well-being.

Financial freedom is not just about accumulating wealth or material possessions. It's about having the ability to live a fulfilling and meaningful life, free from financial stress or constraints. It's about being able to make choices that align with one's personal goals and values, without being limited by financial worries.

In the following chapters, we will explore the strategies and principles that can help individuals achieve financial freedom, regardless of their current financial situation. Whether you're just starting out on your journey to financial success, or you're looking to take your finances to the next level, the principles and strategies in this book will provide you with a roadmap for achieving your financial goals and living a life of true financial freedom.

In order to achieve financial freedom, it's important to understand the different factors that contribute to financial success. These include:

1. **Income:** Having a stable and sufficient source of income is essential for achieving financial freedom. This can come from a job, a business, or investments.

2. **Spending:** Managing expenses and living within your means is crucial for building wealth and achieving financial freedom. This involves creating a budget, tracking expenses, and minimizing unnecessary spending.

3. **Saving:** Building a strong savings habit is critical for achieving financial freedom. This involves setting financial goals, creating a savings plan, and consistently putting money away.

4. Investing: Investing in assets such as stocks, real estate, and mutual funds can help grow wealth and generate passive income.

5. **Debt management:** Managing debt effectively is important for achieving financial freedom. This

involves understanding the different types of debt, creating a plan to pay it off, and avoiding taking on too much debt in the future.

6. **Mindset:** Having a positive and proactive mindset is essential for achieving financial success. This involves being willing to take risks, learning from failures, and being persistent in the pursuit of financial goals.

By understanding these factors and developing a plan that addresses each of them, individuals can create a roadmap to financial freedom. While the path to financial freedom may not be easy, it is achievable for anyone who is willing to put in the work and make the necessary changes to their financial habits and mindset.

Personal stories of individuals who have achieved financial freedom

One such individual is Mark, who grew up in a low-income family and struggled to make ends meet throughout his childhood. Despite the financial challenges he faced, Mark had a strong desire to succeed and worked tirelessly to achieve his goals.

After graduating from college, Mark started his own business selling products online. He spent countless hours building his website, creating marketing campaigns, and optimizing his sales funnel. It was a long and difficult journey, but eventually, Mark's hard work paid off. His business began to grow, and he was able to generate a stable source of income for himself.

As his income grew, Mark started to focus on building his savings and investing in stocks and real estate. He was diligent about saving a portion of his income each month, and he worked with financial advisors to create a sound investment strategy.

Over time, Mark's investments grew, and he was able to generate passive income from his assets. This allowed him to achieve a level of financial freedom that he had never thought possible. He was able to retire early and focus on his passions, traveling the world and giving back to his community.

Another individual who achieved financial freedom is Sarah, who grew up in a middle-class family but struggled with debt throughout her adult life. Despite having a good job and a solid income, Sarah found herself buried in credit card debt and struggling to make ends meet.

Determined to turn her financial situation around, Sarah created a strict budget, cut back on unnecessary expenses, and started paying off her debt aggressively. She also began to focus on building her savings and investing in stocks and mutual funds.

Over time, Sarah's financial situation improved dramatically. She was able to pay off her debt, build a substantial savings account, and generate passive income from her investments. She was no longer living paycheck to paycheck, and she was able to achieve a level of financial security and freedom that she had never thought possible.

These are just a few examples of the many individuals who have achieved financial freedom through hard work, determination, and smart financial habits. By following the strategies and techniques outlined in this book, you too can achieve your financial goals and live a life of true financial freedom.

Another inspiring story of an individual who achieved financial freedom is James, who grew up in poverty and worked multiple jobs to support himself and his family. Despite the challenges he faced, James had a strong work ethic and a burning desire to succeed.

After years of working multiple jobs, James saved enough money to start his own business. He launched a small consulting firm, leveraging his expertise and industry connections to grow his client base. Over time, James' business grew, and he was able to hire a team of employees to help him manage his workload.

As his business grew, James became increasingly focused on building his wealth and achieving financial freedom. He invested in real estate, stocks, and other assets, carefully diversifying his portfolio to minimize risk and maximize returns.

Over time, James' investments grew, and he was able to generate significant passive income from his assets. He was no longer dependent on his consulting business for income, and he was able to retire early and focus on his hobbies and passions.

Another individual who achieved financial freedom is Maria, who grew up in a low-income family and struggled to make ends meet throughout her childhood. Despite the challenges she faced, Maria had a strong desire to succeed and was determined to build a better life for herself and her family.

After graduating from college, Maria landed a high-paying job in finance. She was diligent about saving a portion of her income each month and investing in stocks and other assets. She also started a side hustle, creating and selling handmade crafts online.

Over time, Maria's investments grew, and her side hustle turned into a full-fledged business. She was able to quit her job and focus on her business full-time, generating a stable source of income and achieving financial freedom.

These stories demonstrate that financial freedom is achievable, no matter what your background or current financial situation may be. With hard work, determination, and smart financial habits, you too can achieve your financial goals and live a life of true financial freedom.

Another individual who achieved financial freedom is John, who grew up in a middle-class family and went on to study business in college. After graduation, John landed a job at a Fortune 500 company, where he worked for several years and climbed the corporate ladder.

Despite his success in the corporate world, John had a burning desire to build his own business and achieve financial freedom. He spent years studying entrepreneurship, attending seminars and networking events, and saving money to invest in his own venture.

Eventually, John quit his corporate job and launched his own business, a tech startup that aimed to revolutionize the way people worked and collaborated online. He poured all of his savings and energy into the venture, working tirelessly to develop the product and secure funding from investors.

Over time, John's startup grew, and he was able to attract top talent to his team and secure lucrative partnerships with major corporations. He also invested in other assets, such as real estate and stocks, to diversify his portfolio and maximize his returns.

Today, John is a multi-millionaire and a well-respected entrepreneur in his industry. He has achieved financial freedom and is able to live a life of his choosing, free from the constraints of a 9-to-5 job or financial insecurity.

These stories highlight the importance of taking risks and pursuing your passions in order to achieve financial freedom. Whether you come from poverty or privilege, building wealth and achieving financial independence requires hard work, dedication, and a willingness to take calculated risks. By following the strategies and examples outlined in this book, you too can overcome the challenges and achieve the financial freedom you deserve.

Strategies for achieving financial freedom through passive income, retirement planning, and wealth management

Achieving financial freedom is not just about building wealth, but also about managing it effectively to ensure long-term stability and security. Here are some strategies for achieving financial freedom:

1. **Passive income:** Generating passive income is a great way to achieve financial freedom. Passive income refers to income generated without active involvement, such as through rental properties, dividends from stocks, or royalties from creative works. By building multiple streams of passive income, you can create a stable and reliable source of income that can help you achieve financial freedom.

2. **Retirement planning:** Retirement planning is essential for achieving financial freedom. This involves setting aside a portion of your income each month towards your retirement fund, whether

through a 401(k), IRA, or other retirement account. By starting early and consistently contributing to your retirement fund, you can ensure that you have enough savings to support yourself in your retirement years.

Living a life that is in alignment with one's values and priorities is a crucial aspect of overall well-being and happiness. It involves identifying and understanding what is truly important to you and making intentional choices and actions that reflect those values and priorities. This can help bring a sense of purpose and meaning to your life, and reduce stress and anxiety that may come from living a life that is not aligned with your true self.

To achieve this, it's important to take time for self-reflection and self-discovery. This can involve exploring your beliefs, desires, and passions, and identifying what truly matters to you. Once you have a clear understanding of your values and priorities, you can begin to make intentional choices in all areas of your life, including your career, relationships, and financial decisions.

Living a life that is in alignment with your values and priorities may also involve setting boundaries and saying "no" to things that do not serve you or align with your goals. This can be challenging, but it's important to remember that by prioritizing what truly matters to you, you can create a more fulfilling and satisfying life.

Overall, living a life that is in alignment with one's values and priorities is an ongoing process of self-discovery and intentional action. By making choices that reflect your true self, you can experience greater happiness, purpose, and fulfillment.

3. **Wealth management:** Managing your wealth effectively is crucial for achieving financial freedom. This involves creating a diversified investment portfolio that includes a mix of stocks, bonds, real estate, and other assets. It also involves minimizing debt and living within your means to ensure that you are not overspending or accumulating unnecessary debt.

Wealth management is the process of strategically managing one's financial resources to achieve long-term financial goals. Effective wealth management requires a comprehensive understanding of personal finance, investment strategies, and risk management.

To manage wealth effectively, individuals should start by creating a budget to understand their income, expenses, and savings. From there, they can create a plan for their investments, which should be diversified across multiple asset classes to mitigate risk and maximize returns. This may involve consulting with financial professionals, such as financial advisors or wealth managers, to create a personalized investment plan that aligns with their financial goals and risk tolerance.

In addition to investment management, effective wealth management also involves minimizing debt and living within one's means. This may include creating a plan to pay off high-interest debt, such as credit card debt, and avoiding unnecessary expenses that could impact long-term financial goals. By managing debt effectively and living within their means, individuals can ensure that their wealth is being allocated towards investments and financial goals, rather than towards paying off debt.

Overall, effective wealth management involves a proactive approach to managing one's finances and investments, with a focus on minimizing risk and maximizing returns over the long term.

4. **Budgeting:** Budgeting is an important tool for achieving financial freedom. By creating a budget and tracking your expenses, you can identify areas where you can cut back on spending and save more money. This can help you build your savings and achieve your financial goals faster.

Budgeting is a process of creating a spending plan that helps you manage your income and expenses effectively. It involves tracking your income and expenses and then allocating your money towards different categories such as housing, food, transportation, entertainment, and savings. By creating a budget, you can get a clear picture of your financial situation, set financial goals, and develop a plan to achieve those goals.

One of the key benefits of budgeting is that it can help you identify areas where you may be overspending or wasting money. For example, you may be spending too much money on eating out or subscriptions that you don't use. By tracking your expenses and creating a budget, you can identify these areas and make adjustments to your spending habits.

Budgeting also helps you prioritize your expenses and ensure that you are allocating your money towards your most important financial goals. For example, if your goal is to save for a down payment on a house, you can allocate a portion of your income towards savings each month.

In addition, budgeting can help you avoid accumulating unnecessary debt. By living within your means and allocating your money towards your most important expenses, you can avoid overspending and accumulating credit card debt or other types of debt that can hold you back from achieving financial freedom.

Overall, budgeting is an essential tool for achieving financial freedom. By creating a spending plan and sticking to it, you can manage your finances effectively, identify areas for improvement, and make progress towards your financial goals.

5. **Seeking professional advice**: Finally, seeking professional advice from a financial advisor or wealth manager can be helpful in achieving financial freedom. These professionals can provide guidance on investment strategies, retirement planning, and other financial issues, helping you make informed decisions and maximize your wealth-building potential.

6. **Developing a growth mindset:** A growth mindset is the belief that your abilities and skills can be developed through hard work and dedication. Adopting a growth mindset can help you stay motivated and resilient in the face of financial challenges, and can help you develop the skills and knowledge needed to build wealth and achieve financial freedom.

7. **Avoiding common financial pitfalls:** There are many common financial pitfalls that can derail your efforts to achieve financial freedom, such as overspending, accumulating debt, or failing to save for emergencies. By being aware of these pitfalls and taking steps to avoid them, such as living within your means and building an emergency fund, you can stay on track towards your financial goals.

8. **Building a strong support network:** Building a strong support network of friends, family, and mentors can be invaluable in achieving financial freedom. Your support network can provide encouragement, guidance, and accountability as you work towards

your goals, and can help you stay motivated and focused when times get tough.

9. **Continually learning and growing:** Finally, continually learning and growing is essential for achieving financial freedom. This involves staying up-to-date on the latest investment strategies, financial trends, and wealth-building techniques, and continuously seeking out new opportunities to expand your knowledge and skills. By staying curious and open-minded, you can build the foundation for long-term financial success and achieve true financial freedom.

Summary of the book's key points

In summary, "From Rags to Riches: The Journey to Wealth" is a comprehensive guide to achieving financial freedom and building wealth. The book begins by defining poverty and its impact on individuals and communities, and then explores personal stories of individuals who have overcome poverty and achieved success.

The book also defines wealth and the different forms it can take, and provides personal stories of individuals who have built wealth through entrepreneurship, investing, and saving. It offers practical strategies for overcoming common challenges faced by those seeking wealth, including developing a growth mindset and avoiding financial pitfalls.

The book also defines financial freedom and provides personal stories of individuals who have achieved it. It offers strategies for achieving financial freedom through passive income, retirement planning, and wealth management.

Throughout the book, the importance of developing a strong support network and continually learning and growing is emphasized. By following the strategies outlined in this book, readers can build a solid foundation for achieving long-term financial success and true financial freedom.

In addition to the key points outlined above, the book also emphasizes the importance of taking action and being proactive in pursuing financial goals. It encourages readers to create a plan for achieving their desired level of wealth and to consistently take steps towards that plan.

The book also explores the role of mindset in achieving success and building wealth. It highlights the importance of developing a growth mindset, cultivating a positive attitude, and avoiding negative self-talk or limiting beliefs that may hold individuals back.

Furthermore, the book touches on the idea of giving back and the importance of using wealth to make a positive impact on others and the world. It encourages readers to consider the potential for philanthropy and social responsibility in their financial goals.

Overall, "From Rags to Riches: The Journey to Wealth" offers practical guidance and inspiring stories for anyone seeking to overcome poverty and achieve financial freedom. It provides a roadmap for building wealth through entrepreneurship, investing, and savings, and offers strategies for overcoming common challenges and developing a growth mindset.

Final thoughts on the journey from rags to riches

In conclusion, the journey from rags to riches is not an easy one, but it is achievable for anyone who is willing to put in the effort and take action towards their financial goals. The road may be long and filled with challenges, but with persistence, resilience, and a growth mindset, anyone can achieve financial freedom and create a better life for themselves and their loved ones.

It is important to remember that wealth is not just about accumulating money or material possessions, but also about creating a fulfilling and meaningful life. This can involve giving back to the community, pursuing passions and hobbies, and spending time with loved ones.

The stories of individuals who have overcome poverty and achieved financial success serve as a reminder that anyone can achieve their dreams, regardless of their starting point. By following the strategies outlined in this book, and by remaining committed to their goals, readers can also experience the journey from rags to riches and create a brighter future for themselves and their families.

It is important to note that the strategies and advice presented in this book are not a one-size-fits-all solution. Each person's journey to wealth and financial freedom will be unique, and it is important to tailor these strategies to fit one's individual circumstances and goals.

Furthermore, it is crucial to maintain a long-term perspective and not to become discouraged by setbacks or obstacles along the way. Building wealth and achieving financial freedom is a marathon, not a sprint, and it requires consistent effort and a willingness to learn and adapt.

Ultimately, the journey from rags to riches is about more than just financial success - it is about personal growth, self-discovery, and creating a better life for oneself and one's loved ones. By following the advice and strategies outlined in this book, readers can embark on their own journey to wealth and financial freedom, and experience the many benefits that come with it.

Encouragement and motivation for readers to take action towards building their own wealth

I want to take a moment to offer some final words of encouragement and motivation for readers who are inspired to take action towards building their own wealth.

Remember that the journey to wealth and financial freedom may not be easy, but it is always worth it. By setting clear goals, creating a plan of action, and staying committed to your vision, you can achieve anything you set your mind to.

There will be obstacles and setbacks along the way, but these are simply opportunities for growth and learning.

Use them as stepping stones towards success, rather than allowing them to derail you from your path.

And finally, remember that building wealth and achieving financial freedom is not just about the money. It is about creating a better life for yourself and your loved ones, and having the freedom to pursue your passions and dreams. So don't wait - start taking action towards your own journey from rags to riches today, and see how far you can go!

It is important to also remember that building wealth and achieving financial freedom is not just about yourself - it can also have a positive impact on your community and the world around you.

As you build your own wealth, consider ways in which you can give back and make a difference in the lives of others. This can be through supporting local businesses, donating to charity, or even starting your own philanthropic initiatives.

By using your resources to create positive change in the world, you can not only achieve financial success, but also leave a lasting legacy that will benefit future generations.

So don't be afraid to dream big and pursue your goals with passion and purpose. With hard work, dedication, and a commitment to making a difference, you can achieve anything you set your mind to and create a life of abundance, both for yourself and those around you.